JONAH'S TALE OF A WHALE

By Barry L. Schwartz

Illustrated by James Rey Sanchez

APPLES & HONEY PRESS

In memory of my father, Rudy Schwartz, a compassionate man.
— BLS

To my Emily. You are so kind and graceful. I love you.
— JRS

The illustrations in this book were created with digital tools.

Text copyright © 2021 by Barry L. Schwartz
Illustrations copyright © 2021 by Apples and Honey Press

ISBN 978-1-68115-562-3

Library of Congress Cataloging-in-Publication Data
Names: Schwartz, Barry L., author. | Sanchez, James Rey, illustrator.
Title: Jonah's tale of a whale / Barry L. Schwartz ; illustrated by James
  Rey Sanchez.
Description: Millburn : Apples and Honey Press, [2021] | Audience: Grades
  K-1 | Summary: "A retelling of the biblical tale of Jonah and the
  whale"-- Provided by publisher.
Identifiers: LCCN 2019053251 | ISBN 9781681155623 (hardcover)
Subjects: LCSH: Jonah (Biblical prophet)--Juvenile literature. | Bible
  stories, English--Jonah.
Classification: LCC BS580.J55 S39 2012 | DDC 224/.9209505--dc23
LC record available at https://lccn.loc.gov/2019053251

Design by Annemarie Redmond
Edited by Ann D. Koffsky

Printed in China
9 8 7 6 5 4 3 2 1

onah lived by the sea.
As a boy he heard fishermen tell tales
of whales that swallowed up ships.

ne day, Jonah heard God command:
"Go to the great city of Nineveh and
tell the people, 'Stop acting badly!'"

Even though Jonah was a prophet, God's
messenger, he didn't want to deliver the message.

Jonah was a Jew from Israel. Nineveh was Israel's enemy!

Jonah wanted Nineveh to be *punished*, not saved.

So he took a boat in the opposite direction.

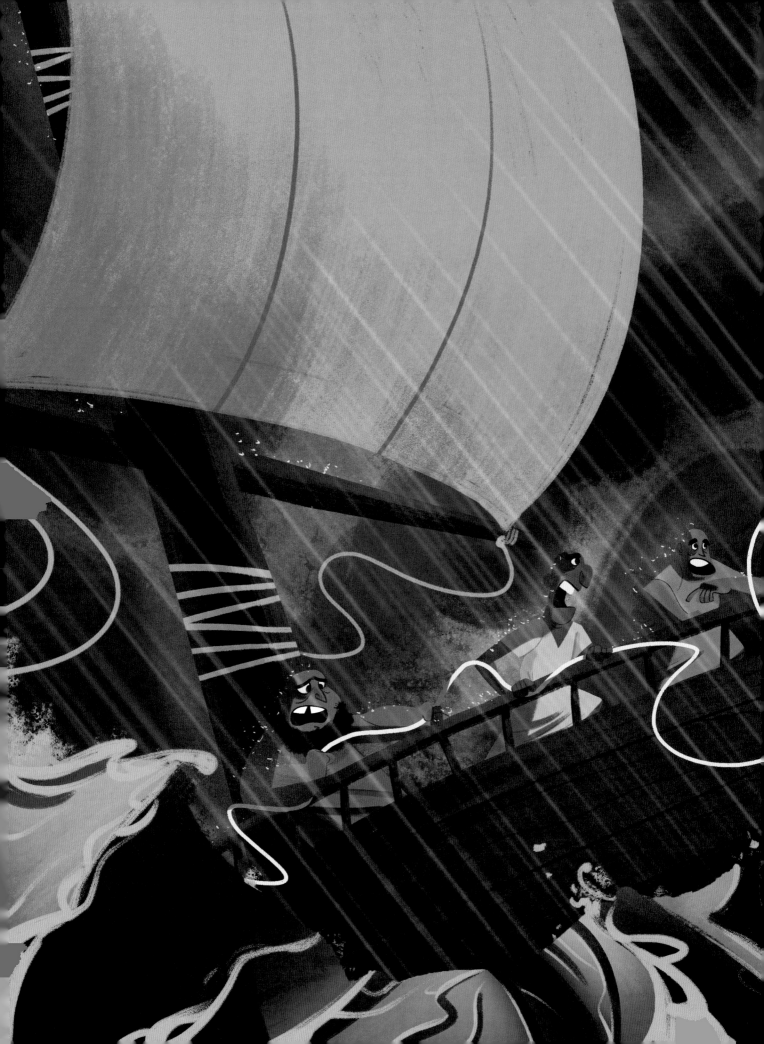

All of a sudden, a great storm arose. Howling wind, pouring rain, and crashing waves washed over the deck.

The sailors cried out to their gods,

"Save us!"

But Jonah went to sleep down below. He even snored.

"Wake up, wake up!" yelled the captain. "How can you be
asleep at a time like this?"

The sailors said to each other, "We must find out who's to blame for this storm."

They gathered pieces of clay and put a mark on one of them. One by one each sailor picked a piece.

Jonah picked the one with the mark. That meant he was to blame!

"Who *are* you?" the sailors asked Jonah. "Where have you come from? Who are your people?"

"I'm from Israel," said Jonah. "This is my fault. God is calling me, but I'm running away. Cast me overboard! I am sure that will calm this storm."

"No way! Just pray," said the sailors, "and grab an oar!"

But the storm grew worse and worse, and finally . . .

. . . the sailors threw Jonah overboard
to save themselves.

The sea became calm.

Jonah floated . . . right into the mouth
of a great gray whale!

onah sat in the belly of the beast three days and three nights.

On day one, Jonah looked for a way out. There was none!

Jonah realized there was no way out of God's command either.

"I can't run away from what I'm supposed to do," Jonah said to himself. "Even if it's hard."

On day two, the ride got bumpy.

Jonah remembered the good-hearted sailors who had tried to save him in the storm.

"If they tried to help me, then I should try to help Nineveh," Jonah thought.

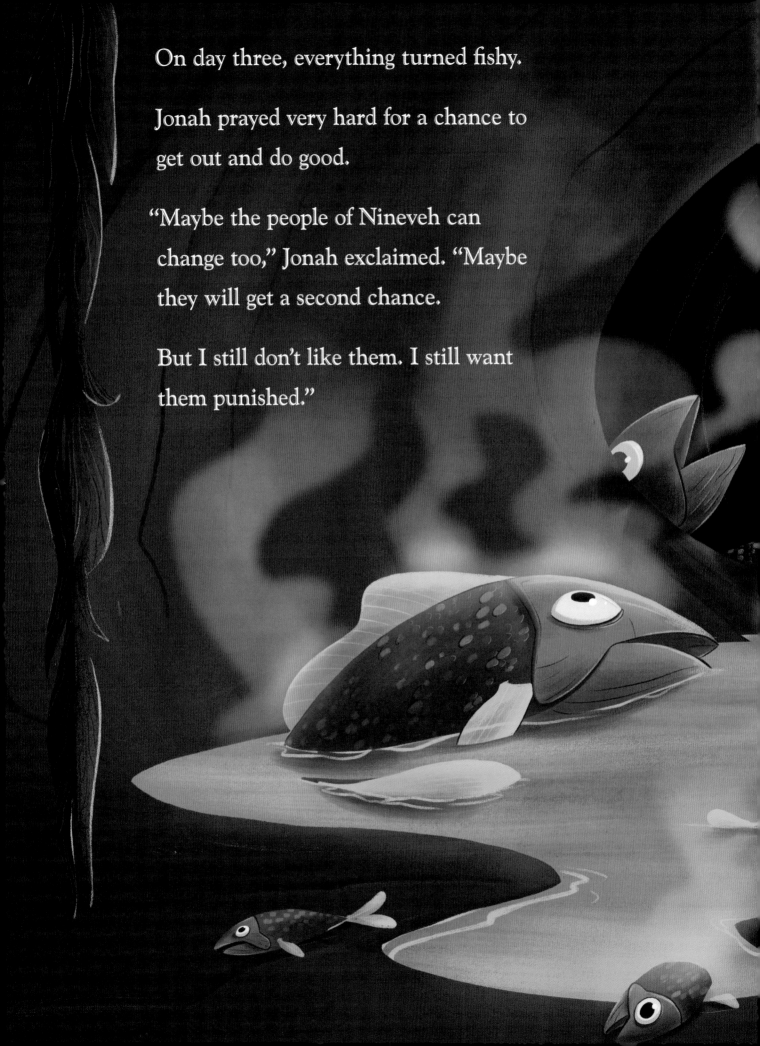

On day three, everything turned fishy.

Jonah prayed very hard for a chance to get out and do good.

"Maybe the people of Nineveh can change too," Jonah exclaimed. "Maybe they will get a second chance.

But I still don't like them. I still want them punished."

As the fourth day dawned, the whale felt funny.

He had an upset stomach and thought it might
be Jonah's fault.

He burped out Jonah onto a beach.

"Thanks," Jonah said to the whale.
"I needed that."

onah heard God command again:
"Go to Nineveh, and tell the
people to change their ways."

This time Jonah listened.

He went around the city declaring, "In forty days, Nineveh will be punished!"

The people of Nineveh paid attention.

Even the king said, "I'm sorry."

Everyone fasted and cried and begged for forgiveness from God and from each other.

Afterward, Jonah wondered: Had their apologies worked? Were the people forgiven?

He went up a hill to see what would happen to Nineveh. Nothing happened.

Life went on as usual, with one big difference. Now the people of Nineveh were nice to one another.

They greeted family, friends, and even strangers with a smile.

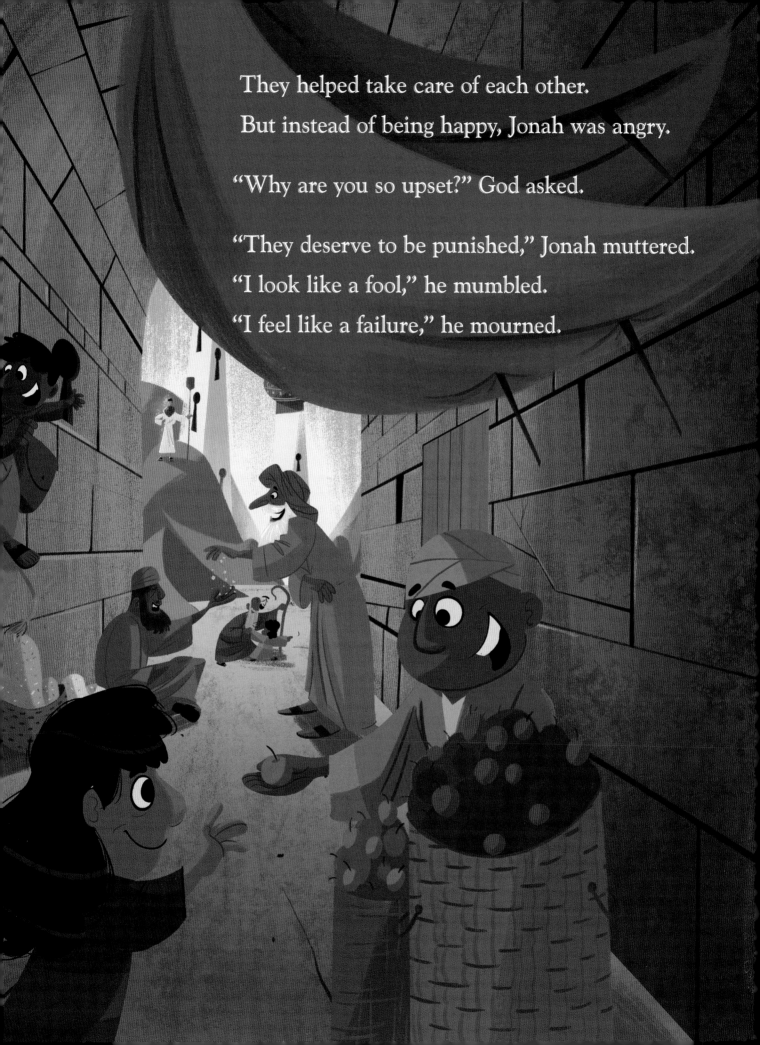

They helped take care of each other.
But instead of being happy, Jonah was angry.

"Why are you so upset?" God asked.

"They deserve to be punished," Jonah muttered.
"I look like a fool," he mumbled.
"I feel like a failure," he mourned.

God was glad the people had changed. But Jonah was still unhappy. He found a leafy tree and rested in its shade.

All of a sudden, the leaves turned yellow and shriveled up, and Jonah became faint from the heat.

"Save this tree!" he yelled.

"Why are you so upset?" God asked. "Do you care more about saving this tree than saving this city? Look at the men, women, and children—even the animals. Shall I not have compassion for them?

Go home now, Jonah. Dare to care and tell your tale."

Jonah went home.
He told his tale of the whale
to anyone who listened.

He told the children about how he ran away . . .
and came back.

He told the sailors about sleeping through a storm . . . and waking up.

He told the townsfolk about how a whole city was saved.

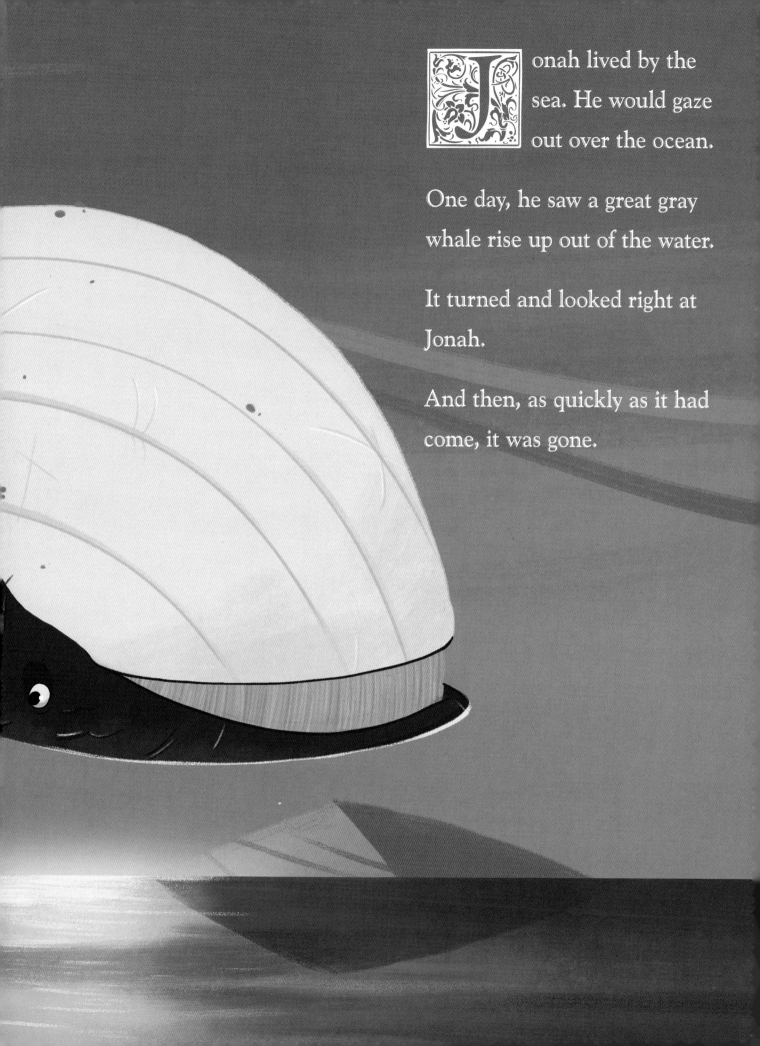

Jonah lived by the sea. He would gaze out over the ocean.

One day, he saw a great gray whale rise up out of the water.

It turned and looked right at Jonah.

And then, as quickly as it had come, it was gone.

A Note for Families

eople do not normally get swallowed by a whale and live to tell the tale! But as fantastical as the book of Jonah's story might seem, the sages saw an important message in it and chose to read it every year on the most holy of days: Yom Kippur.

Nineveh was the capital of the Assyrian Empire, and in biblical times, its people viciously attacked Israel. No wonder Jonah did not want to go there and help Israel's enemy!

Yet Jonah stopped running away and accepted responsibility.

The people of Nineveh listened and learned.

The book of Jonah teaches us that even our enemies may change their ways. Now that is a lesson worth remembering.

We all have stormy journeys, but we can learn from our experiences.

- What new responsibility will you accept, like Jonah?

- Who will you help in a time of need, like the whale?

- How will you be a better person, like the Ninevites?

Always remember to dare to care!

Rabbi Barry L. Schwartz